A line-of-b

HMS *Victory*

the great

achievements of the early

Industrial Revolution

HULL

The hull required nearly 6,000 trees for its construction of which some 90% is oak. The hull is almost **3ft (92cm) thick** near the keel. *Victory* needed a depth of water of just over 24ft (7.3m) to float. In 1780 the area below the waterline was sheathed with 3,923 sheets of copper to protect her hull from ship worm and marine growths. Over half a million copper nails held these 15 tons of copper in place.

THE GREAT GUNS

At the Battle of Trafalgar, *Victory* carried thirty 32-pounder guns, twenty-eight 24-pounders, forty-four 12-pounders and two 68-pounder carronades. A total of **104 guns** capable of firing a broadside of 1,148 lbs (522kg) of shot. With fresh gun crews these could be reloaded in 90 seconds. At the beginning of the battle all her guns, except the carronades were treble-shotted unleashing 1.5 tons of iron! To give the ship stability, the heaviest guns are lowest down, except for the two massive carronades on the forecastle.

ROUND SHOT
Penetrated and splintered hulls

CHAIN SHOT
Cut sails and rigging

BAR SHOT
Broke yards and masts

GRAPE SHOT
Anti-personnel

POOP DECK & MASTS

The poop deck provided an **elevated viewpoint**. It was used for **controlling the sails** on the mizzen and main masts and for **signalling**. The space under the forward edge provided protection for the wheel and helmsmen.

Like all large ships of her time, *Victory* relied on wind power to move. The driving force on the sails was transmitted to the masts and down into her hull. Skilled handling of the sails, by means of ropes, enabled the direction of travel of the ship to be controlled and even allowed her to stop without dropping anchor.

MASTS

Each of the masts is made up of three overlapping sections. The upper masts could be raised or lowered at sea for repair or in bad weather.

TOPS

These platforms are fixed at the top of the lower masts. Apart from their use for the attachment of rigging they also provided an elevated viewpoint and position for firing muskets and throwing grenades and stink pots onto the deck of an enemy ship.

FEATURE
SIGNALLING

Daytime communication between ships and the shore was by means of signalling flags.

The Popham code meant that the flags, used in different combinations, could produce about 12,000 basic words and sentences.

Before the Battle of Trafalgar, Nelson's famous signal *England expects that every man will do his duty* was sent as individual hoists of up to 3 flags. For example 'England' is made up of flags 2, 5 & 3, while duty had to be spelt out letter by letter. Lights and false fires were used to signal at night.

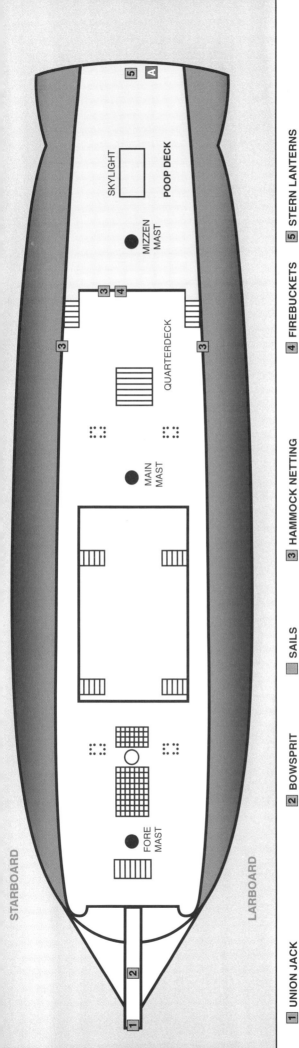

STARBOARD

LARBOARD

SKYLIGHT

POOP DECK

MIZZEN MAST

QUARTERDECK

MAIN MAST

FORE MAST

1 UNION JACK

At anchor, the Union flag - Great Britain's national flag - is flown from the jack staff. Only there is it known as the Union Jack.

2 BOWSPRIT

Effectively a fourth mast extending from the bows of the ship.

SAILS

Victory carried 37 sails providing a sail area of 5,468 m².

3 HAMMOCK NETTING

Hammocks were tightly stowed in the nets during the day. In action they provided protection from small arms fire.

4 FIREBUCKETS

Made of leather and filled with sand or water.

5 STERN LANTERNS

At night these three lanterns, which burned whale oil, enabled ships to keep in formation and to avoid collisions.

QUARTERDECK, WAIST & FORECASTLE

From the stern to just forward of the main mast is the quarterdeck. This was the **nerve centre of the ship** from where Captain Hardy controlled the ship and Vice-Admiral Lord Nelson commanded the British fleet at the Battle of Trafalgar.

THE QUARTERDECK

The captain's spacious quarters, which were dismantled and stowed below the waterline in action, were next to the quarterdeck, the command and control centre of the ship.

FEATURE
NELSON'S PLAQUE

This plaque A marks the spot where, at about 1.15pm on 21 October 1805, Vice-Admiral Lord Nelson fell wounded. He had been shot by a sharpshooter stationed in the mizzen top of the French ship *Rédoutable* during the Battle of Trafalgar.

THE WAIST

This is the area over which the boats are stored. It used to be open with the gangways, linking the quarterdeck and forecastle, on each side.

THE FORECASTLE

The work necessary for stowing the anchor was carried out on this deck. From here the sails and yards on the main and fore masts, as well as the bowsprit, were also controlled. At Trafalgar, the opening shot of *Victory's* first broadside was fired by the larboard carronade B which delivered its devastating load of a single 68-pound shot and 500 musket balls through the vulnerable stern of the *Bucentaure*, killing and wounding nearly 200 men and upending 20 guns.

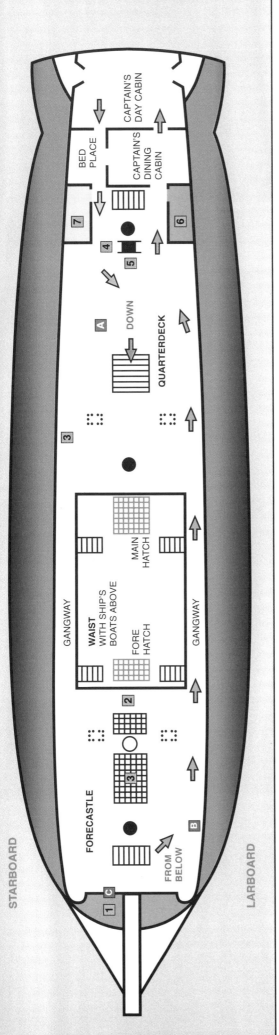

STARBOARD

LARBOARD

FORECASTLE

FROM BELOW

WAIST
WITH SHIP'S
BOATS ABOVE

GANGWAY

FORE HATCH

MAIN HATCH

GANGWAY

QUARTERDECK

DOWN

BED PLACE

CAPTAIN'S DAY CABIN

CAPTAIN'S DINING CABIN

1 HEAD
Forward of the beakhead bulkhead **C**, it contains the heads (lavatories).

2 BELFRY
A varying number of 'bells' was rung every half hour to indicate the time.

3 GRATINGS
Cover openings in the deck and provided ventilation. Seamen were seized up to them to be flogged.

4 WHEEL
Connected by a rope to the tiller on the lower gun deck.

5 BINNACLE
Houses two compasses and a lanthorn to illuminate them at night.

6 MASTER'S CABIN
The master was responsible for the sailing and navigation of the ship.

7 SECRETARY'S CABIN
The admiral's secretary was an important position and he needed to be at hand.

UPPER GUN DECK

Often referred to as the main deck, the upper gun deck carried thirty **long 12-pounder guns.** It was the main **working deck** where sails were mended, the carpenter and his mates worked as well as where a host of other essential activities were carried out.

SICK BERTH

The sick berth and dispensary are situated near fresh air and the heads. On a damp crowded ship diseases and fevers were common. Long periods at sea added to the problem. Injuries were not just the result of battle, but happened during the day-to-day running of the ship. Around the time of the Battle of Trafalgar, 80% of deaths in the navy were as a result of disease, accidents and shipwrecks. In action, the sick berth was relocated on the orlop.

FEATURE
THE WORKING DECK

Day-to-day maintenance and repairs were carried out on this deck. Although the centre section below the boats - the waist - was open to the elements, there was shelter and space around it for the sailmaker, carpenter and their crews to work.

ADMIRAL'S QUARTERS

Home to many famous admirals, these cabins have been linked to Vice-Admiral Lord Nelson ever since the Battle of Trafalgar. When cleared for action all this finery was dismantled and removed to the safety of the hold.

The airy day cabin is separated from the dining cabin by bulkheads which hinge up. Forward on the starboard side is the admiral's bedplace. The cot is similar to that used by Nelson and the wash cabinet is over 200 years old. The admiral's heads (lavatories) were housed in the elegant quarter galleries A at the stern. Portable flushing water closets may have been used by the officers.

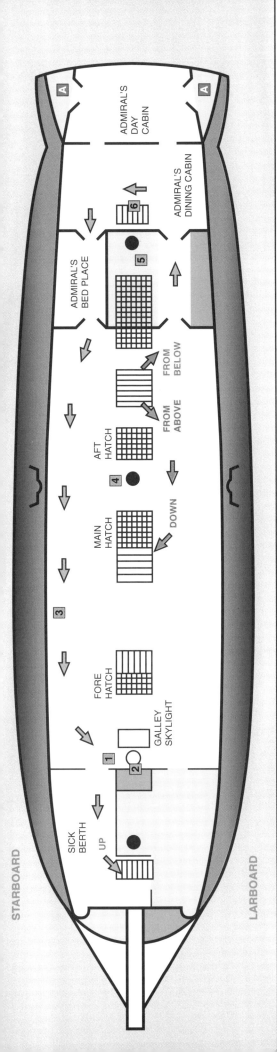

STARBOARD

LARBOARD

A | A
ADMIRAL'S DAY CABIN
ADMIRAL'S DINING CABIN
ADMIRAL'S BED PLACE
6
5
AFT HATCH
4
FROM ABOVE
FROM BELOW
MAIN HATCH
DOWN
FORE HATCH
3
GALLEY SKYLIGHT
1
2
SICK BERTH
UP

1 CHICKEN COOPS
Hens provided fresh eggs for the officers. Larger animals were penned towards the bows.

2 VENT & FLUE
The steam vent let the steam from cooking rise up through the gratings above. Smoke escaped up the flue.

3 BILBOES or LEG IRONS
For minor offenders, or those awaiting more serious punishment. A 'cat o' nine tails' hangs nearby.

4 ELM TREE PUMPS
Pumped seawater under pressure onto the ship for fire-fighting and washing both the ship and crew.

5 STEERAGE
Here the admiral's servants worked, ate and slept. The cask containing Nelson's body was placed here after Trafalgar.

6 LADDER
For quick access a ladder led up to the quarterdeck.

MIDDLE GUN DECK

Primarily a gun deck, which housed the **24-pounder guns**, the **galley** was situated on this deck. The **Royal Marine detachment** lived in the deck space forward of the **officers' quarters** which occupied the stern.

FEATURE
A SQUARE MEAL

It was important that the crew was well fed and healthy. Three meals a day comprising a high protein diet of over 4,000 calories gave the men the energy to carry out the hard physical work. Fresh food and lime juice were used when available.

If the food supplied to the ship was bad, or went off, it was condemned by three officers and returned for reimbursement or thrown overboard.

THE GALLEY

Food was **cooked** on the coal and wood burning stove, whose condenser A also provided some fresh water. Two large coppers were used for boiling the bags of food prepared by each mess. The ovens were for baking bread and the grate, spit and hanging stoves B for cooking the officer's food.

A TYPICAL DAY'S FOOD

For breakfast, a rough porridge - burgoo. Lunch was usually salted meat and/or dried peas. Supper was the leftovers from lunch or cheese with ship's biscuit known as bread (the origin of today's biscuits). As the water was unpalatable, 8 pints of beer, 2 pints of wine or 0.5 pints of rum were issued each day. This diet was similar to, if not better than, that eaten by people on land.

CAPSTANS

Victory has two double capstans which extend between two decks. These enormous winches were used for **hauling in ropes and cables**. A double capstan enabled the cable to be wound round the capstan on one deck, out of the way of the men working the capstan bars on the other deck. The **jeer capstan C** was used for hoisting masts, yards, boats, guns and stores. The **main capstan D** was used for hauling in the anchor; 260 men working both upper and lower parts could lift up to 10 tons.

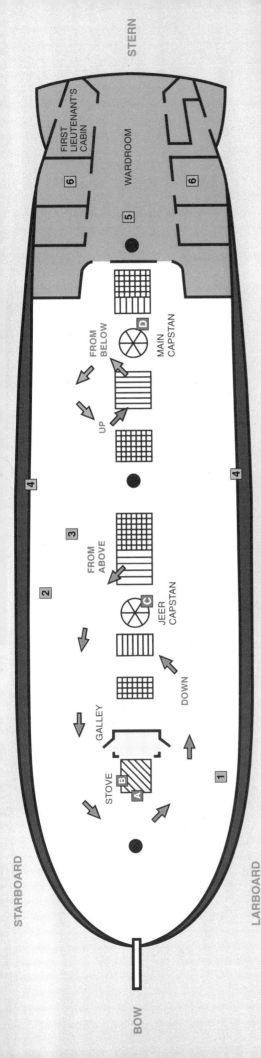

STERN

STARBOARD

BOW

LARBOARD

FIRST LIEUTENANT'S CABIN

6 WARDROOM 6

5

FROM BELOW

MAIN CAPSTAN

UP

FROM ABOVE

3

2

4

4

JEER CAPSTAN

DOWN

GALLEY

STOVE

B
A

1

1 24-POUNDER GUNS

This original gun weighs 2.5 tons. It fired a 24 lb / 10.9kg shot over a mile in distance.

2 ROYAL MARINES QUARTERS

The volunteer, loyal and well-disciplined Royal Marines ate and slept here, forming a barrier between the crew and officers.

3 PAINT & COLOURS

The limewash sides down here reflected what little light there was and eliminated bacteria.

4 ENTRY PORTS

These were only used by the admiral, captain and important visitors.

5 WARDROOM

The senior officers ate and relaxed here; separated from the rest of the ship by a removable wooden bulkhead.

6 OFFICERS' CABINS

These were shared with guns. In action the 'walls' were taken down and the contents stored in the hold.

LOWER GUN DECK

This deck, with its original oak planking, carried the formidable **32-pounder guns**. It was also the main **living quarters** for the **crew** and the level at which the **anchor cable** entered the ship. Dark, crowded and poorly ventilated the smell of the lower gun deck must have been overpowering.

MESSENGERS

The main anchor cables were too thick to pass around a capstan, so a thinner endless 'messenger' rope A was married to the cable by short lengths of rope called 'nippers'. When the main capstan B was rotated, the messenger moved, dragging the cable with it. At the point where the cable dropped down to the orlop the nippers were removed and re-attached further forward.

FEATURE
CLEAR FOR ACTION

The larboard (port) side of this deck has been cleared for action. The 90 mess tables for 580 men, which were placed across the deck, hatches and between the guns, had to be removed, as would anything that would obstruct the guns. Fire hoses were laid along the deck, which would have been wetted and sprinkled with sand to deactivate any loose powder.

HAMMOCKS

480 hammocks were slung on this deck and possibly at different heights to give more space. Each seaman had a wool mattress, pillow and two blankets. During the day, they were rolled up and stored in the hammock nettings on deck.

GUNROOM

The living quarters of the gunner, chaplain and junior officers.

TILLER

The 29 foot long tiller C swung in a broad arc across the deckhead. After the wheel had been shot away at the Battle of Trafalgar, Victory was steered from here.

STARBOARD

BOW

STERN

LARBOARD

GUNROOM

C

FROM BELOW

EXIT

B

3

UP

A

FROM ABOVE

DOWN

3

RIDING BITTS

2

2

FREEFLOW ENTRANCE

1

4 5

4 4

1 MANGER

The low bulkhead stopped seawater flowing along the deck. The area was used for hosing the anchor cable as it came on-board and occasionally for restraining small animals.

2 RIDING BITTS

Once the anchor had been dropped, the cable was attached to these timbers.

3 CAPSTANS

The lower parts of the double capstans which extend between two decks.

4 CHAIN PUMPS

Stopped the ship sinking. A continuous chain with leather washers could pump out up to 30 tons of water per hour from the bottom of the ship.

5 ELM TREE PUMPS

Hoses could be attached at this level to provide a supply of sea water for use on board.

ORLOP

This deck provided space for **stores** that needed to be accessible. Being **below the waterline** it was relatively safe in battle; there are two **powder magazines** on this level and the **emergency operating area**. It was on the orlop that Vice-Admiral **Lord Nelson died** during the Battle of Trafalgar.

DEATH OF NELSON

After he had been shot Lord Nelson was carried down to the orlop where he died at 4.30pm on 21 October 1805. **F**

Where exactly did he die?

See HMS Victory CD-ROM

AFTER COCKPIT

In action it was taken over and transformed into an operating theatre for the ship's surgeon. The area aft of the sail room provided quarters for the midshipmen and master's mates.

HANGING MAGAZINES

To avoid confusion each magazine only stored one size of powder cartridge. Entry was past a damp woollen 'fearnought' curtain. To prevent sparks, the magazines were lined with copper and lead. Light came from separate light rooms **E**. The magazines were suspended over the hold to allow ventilation.

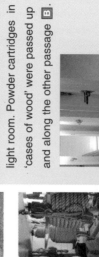

STORES

The carpenter's **C** and boatswain's stores **D** made the ship virtually self-reliant.

FEATURE
PASSAGES

To prevent fire these unlit passages, which give the only access to the grand magazine below, have white plaster walls and lead floors.

Empty cases of wood were returned along the light room passage **A** which also led to the light room. Powder cartridges in 'cases of wood' were passed up and along the other passage **B**.

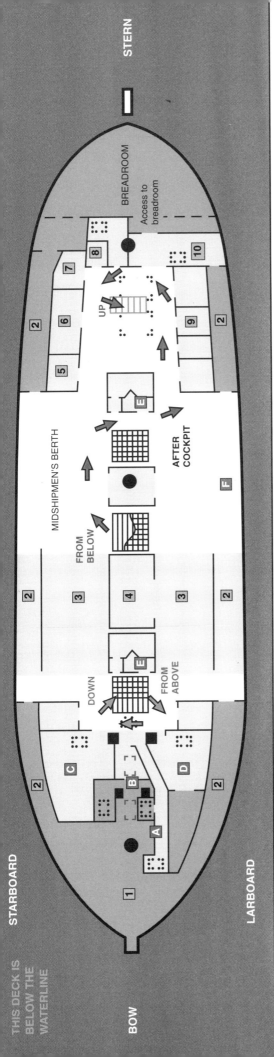

STARBOARD

STERN

BOW

LARBOARD

THIS DECK IS BELOW THE WATERLINE

BREADROOM

Access to breadroom

UP

MIDSHIPMEN'S BERTH

FROM BELOW

AFTER COCKPIT

E

FROM ABOVE

DOWN

E

F

1 GUNNER'S STORE ROOM
Stored parts for the guns and small arms. It was also used by the armourer as a workshop.

2 WING PASSAGES
Enabled the carpenter to repair shot holes below the waterline without moving stores.

3 CABLE TIER
The slatted floor let water from the stored anchor cable drain into the bilges.

4 SAIL ROOM
Next to the main hatch, the sails were stored on racks to prevent mildew.

5 LIEUTENANTS' STORE ROOM
6 CAPTAIN'S STORE ROOM
7 SURGEON'S CABIN
8 DISPENSARY

9 SLOP ROOM
Clothes, bedding and tobacco were sold by the purser, at a profit!

10 STEWARD'S ROOM
Daily rations were issued from here.

THE HOLD

Used for long term **storage** and for heavy items that had to be stowed low down to maintain the ship's stability. As well as provisions and water for 850 men for up to 6 months, there were stores and spare items for the ship itself. Being a fighting ship this included the **safe storage of gunpowder.**

These barrels represent 10% of the 7.5 tons of gunpowder used by *Victory* at Trafalgar

FEATURE

THE GRAND MAGAZINE

Lined with lead, copper and plaster to protect the 35 tons of gunpowder from sparks and rats, its only access was from the passages on the orlop. Over 750 gunpowder barrels were stored on the pallating flat **A**, which is raised off the bottom of the hold. Charcoal was placed under the flat to absorb moisture. Stanchions with battens **B** divide the magazine from the filling room. Gunpowder was tipped into the hopper **C** over which the cartridge bags were filled before being stored on the racks **D**. The only light came from two lanthorns placed behind protective glass and copper grills **E**.

THE PUMP WELL

Reaching into the bilges, near the main mast **F**, are the chain pumps **G**, used for pumping water out of the ship. Elm tree pumps **H** connect to the outside to pump seawater onboard.

CONSTRUCTION

Set at right angles to the keel are closely set vertical frames, locked in place by the keelson **I**. They are covered by planking on the outside and can be glimpsed through the vent spaces **J** in the inner planking **K**. The hull is made watertight by caulking; hammering oakum and pitch in the gaps between the outer planks. Massive riders **L** strengthen the hull.

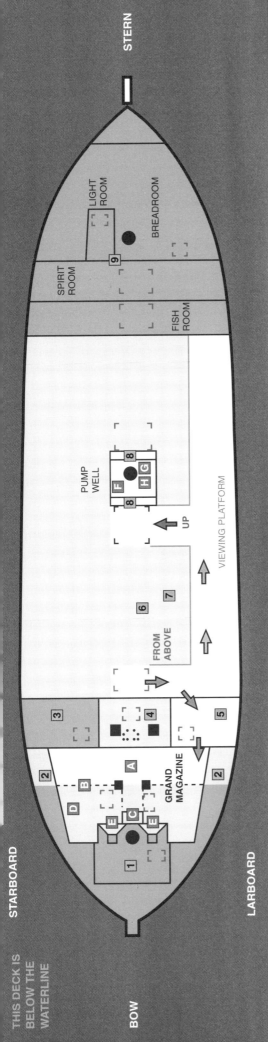

STARBOARD

THIS DECK IS BELOW THE WATERLINE

BOW

LARBOARD

STERN

LIGHT ROOM

SPIRIT ROOM

BREADROOM

FISH ROOM

PUMP WELL

VIEWING PLATFORM

FROM ABOVE

UP

GRAND MAGAZINE

1 LIGHTROOM
Accessed from the orlop, 2 lightboxes illuminate the filling room and magazine.

2 STAVE STORES
Broken-down gunpowder barrels were stored here.

3 CARPENTER'S STORE

4 COAL STORE

5 BOATSWAIN'S STORE

6 CARGO
Casks of water and other provisions were laid on shingle ballast to prevent them moving.

7 BALLAST
To give the ship stability, shingle and 210 tons of iron bars were laid along the bottom of the hold.

8 SHOT LOCKERS
Low down in the ship because of the weight of the 120 tons of shot.

9 AFT STORES
Ship's biscuits, flour and spirits were stored in this area, lit from a light room to avoid explosion.

HISTORY

1759
Victory's keel laid down at Chatham. Designed by Thomas Slade, she is the 6th ship to bear the name.

1759
'Annus Mirabilis' - year of victories. 'Heart of Oak' written.

1778
Fitted out for service and commissioned. Flagship of Admiral Keppel at indecisive **Battle off Ushant** against 30 French ships. Minor repairs needed.

1787-8
Major repairs at Portsmout[h]

1789-92
Served wit[h] the Channe[l] fleet.

1792-3
Refit. Armamer[t] increased

1756-63 Seven Years War **1789-95 French Revolutio[n]**

1765
7 May, Victory launched. Put into reserve.

1771
In danger of sinking. Rushed into dry dock. Repaired and returned to moorings.

1782
Relief of Gibraltar under flag of Admiral Lord Howe.

1781
Battle of Ushant under flag of Rear-Admiral Kempenfelt. Successful action against the French.

1780
Hull sheathed with copper.

Nelson's Victory at the BATTLE OF TRAFALGAR

HMS *Victory* was Lord Nelson's flagship when, despite the courage of the French and Spanish, he inflicted a shattering defeat on their combined fleet off the south-west coast of Spain.

The dogged pursuit and blockade by British naval vessels had finally ended Napoleon's plans to invade Britain. He then moved his victorious troops eastwards to a new theatre of war. The supporting combined fleet, of 18 French and 15 Spanish 'line of battle' ships, was intercepted off Cape Trafalgar by the British fleet of 27 ships.

Tactics

Instead of forming a traditional line of battle parallel to the enemy fleet, Nelson divided his force into two columns which attacked at right angles. The idea was to split the enemy fleet into three and overcome each group individually.